Prepared by Department of the I
on behalf of the Secretary of Sta

Paratowyd gan Adran yr Am
ar ran Ysgrifennydd Gwlado

TINTERN ABBEY

GWENT

ABATY TYNDYRN

O. E. CRASTER   TD, MA, FSA

Inspector of Ancient Monuments

LONDON

HER MAJESTY'S STATIONERY OFFICE

The monument stands on the right bank of the River Wye at the south end of the village of Tintern. It is just off road A466, 5 miles north of Chepstow and 11 miles south of Monmouth. Ordnance Survey 1:50 000 map 162; 1in map 155; reference SO 532998

Front cover design by W Brouard

© *Crown copyright* 1964
First published 1960
Second edition 1964
Seventh impression 1976

ISBN 0 11 670063 7

Tintern Abbey

Drawing by Samuel and Nathaniel Buck dated 1732; the north wall of the nave omitted, to show the interior

Historical Background

The ideal of withdrawing from worldly affairs and concentrating on the worship of God is many thousand years old. The western monastic system developed from the grouping together of solitary hermits. Its beginning can be traced back to the fourth century AD when monasteries began to spring up in countries on the shores of the Mediterranean. This new movement flowered in Wales in the sixth century. Here a number of famous missionaries, amongst them St David, St Illtyd, St Teilo and St Cadoc, attracted bands of followers and set up mother churches each with its own community or "clas." The invasion of England by pagan Angles and Saxons delayed the introduction of monasteries into England, but in the year 598 St Augustine founded one at Canterbury. This house followed the set of rules formulated by St Benedict at Monte Cassino in Italy. The Benedictine rule soon came to be accepted by all religious houses in England, including those in the north of Celtic origin. The monasteries in Wales, however, continued to follow their own pattern until the arrival of William the Conqueror. The Normans reorganised the clas at St David's as a cathedral and founded new priories at Monmouth, Chepstow and elsewhere. The old

Celtic clas were swept away, and Wales rejoined the European monastic system. There was as yet no monastery at Tintern: the old religious centre having been at Llandogo some 3 miles higher up the river. The late eleventh and early twelfth centuries saw a movement for monastic reform which produced various new Orders of monks. There was a desire for greater simplicity and austerity, and an emphasis on manual labour. By far the most successful of the new Orders were the Cistercians, who took their name from the abbey founded at Cîteaux in Burgundy in 1098. The Order was held together by a system of mutual inspection, and an annual meeting of all the abbots at Cîteaux. They chose sites away from towns, and farmed on a considerable scale, having a special class of monks, the lay brothers, to carry out this activity.

The Cistercians were popularly known as White Monks, from the unbleached material of their dress, to distinguish them from the older Benedictines or Black Monks.

In the year 1131 in the reign of Henry I (the fourth son of William the Conqueror) a Cistercian abbey was founded at Tintern. Like their first English house, which had been set up at Waverley in Surrey three years earlier, it was colonised by monks from L'Aumône in Normandy, itself a daughter-house of Cîteaux.

The buildings in all medieval monasteries were laid out to much the same plan. The chief building was always the church, and on one side of this were the four covered walks of the cloister placed round a square courtyard. The monks' dormitory, dining hall, kitchen and other buildings normally opened off the cloister in a set pattern.

At Tintern the buildings were originally laid out on a smaller scale than now, and little remains of those erected at the time of the foundation of the abbey. These Norman buildings were largely rebuilt during the thirteenth century. The abbey church itself was entirely rebuilt between 1270 and 1301.

Here for 400 years the monks carried on the worship of God at fixed hours of the day and night. They studied and copied manuscripts in the cloister, they taught the novices, slept in the dormitory, ate in the dining hall, and cared for the sick or elderly brothers in the infirmary. It was a communal life governed by strict rules and routine and dedicated to the service of God.

The completion of the new church was followed in the fourteenth century by the building of the abbot's hall. With its magnificent buildings freshly completed, this was the peak of the abbey's fortunes. The plague known as the Black Death, which swept the country in 1349, drastically altered the economy, and it became impossible to recruit

Air view showing the abbey and River Wye

lay brothers, who had normally outnumbered the monks. Cistercians henceforward became less distinguishable from the Black Monks, and more involved in the worldly affair of running their estates.

It is perhaps not surprising that by Henry VIII's reign (as long after the abbey's foundation as from then until now) some of the original fervour had gone out of monastic life. The King needed money to support the strong central government that the Tudors had set up, and decided to dissolve all monastic houses—those of canons, friars and nuns as well as monks. Tintern Abbey was thus dissolved in 1536. The lead off the roofs was melted down, and the buildings must have become roofless within a few years of the dissolution. During Tudor times Tintern became famous for its brass, iron and wireworks. These were dependent on the water power from the brook that runs into the Wye just north of the abbey precinct; many cottages were built in and around the ruins. In 1901 the site was bought by the Crown from the Duke of Beaufort, the descendant of Henry, Earl of Worcester, to whom it had been granted in 1537. Administration of it was transferred in 1914 to what is now the Department of the Environment. Since then work has been carried out to conserve the abbey ruins and clear them of later encroachments.

Interior of the church looking east

TINTERN
ABBEY

0   50   100
SCALE OF FEET

The church from the south-east

A Tour of the Abbey

The chief points of interest of the various buildings are given below in the order most convenient for visiting. To make it easier to follow the description, the numbers given to the various sections are also shown on the plan on pages 8–9.

1 Visitors enter the abbey through the *outer parlour* within which the modern ticket office now stands. It was here that conversation between monks and laymen could take place, and in medieval times you would probably have got no further.

2 Turning right you pass the remains of the *stair* by which the lay brothers came down from their dormitory to the church for the night-time services.

3 Like them you enter the *church* through the doorway set diagonally in its north-west corner. The church is remarkably complete: apart from its roofs and the tracery and glass from its windows, the most obvious things that are missing are the pillars of the arcade on the north side of the nave. The lay brothers attended services in the nave. Their stalls, or seats, faced inwards backing on walls built between the pillars, and their altar stood in front of a screen between the fourth pair of pillars from the west. A second screen, known as the pulpitum, which stood between the next pair of pillars to the east, was constructed of stone and still in position in 1854. This formed the west end of the

Clerestory windows on the south side of the nave show the change from the use of detached shafts in the jambs that marks the beginning of the second building period

monks' quire, which occupied the first bay of the nave and the crossing —the central area between the four arms of the church. The monks' quire stalls, which were probably arranged in two or three tiers and made of richly carved oak, were placed against screen walls separating the quire from the transepts. It can be seen that the clustered shafts of the two western pillars of the crossing are not carried down to the ground, but rise from corbels in order to leave room for the stalls. The foundations of the first church are marked out on the ground, and show that not only was it on a considerably smaller scale but it was sited further to the north than the building which replaced it in the years following 1270. The whole of the church had stone-vaulted ceilings, as can be seen from the springers that rise from wall-shafts. The vaulting was carried on simple transverse and diagonal ribs with stone bosses at the intersections of the latter. Some of these finely carved bosses are laid out on the ground. When the vaulted ceilings were in position there would have been a large amount of accommodation between the tops of the vaults and the roofs. These roof-spaces were lit by the great

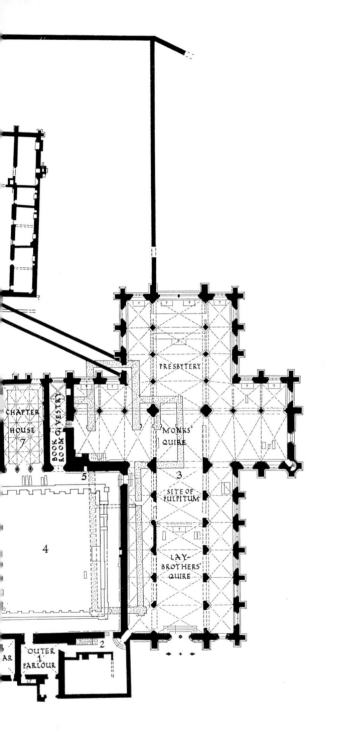

PRESBYTERY

CHAPTER
HOUSE
7

BOOK
ROOM

VESTRY

MONKS'
QUIRE

5

3

SITE OF
PULPITUM

4

LAY-
BROTHERS'
QUIRE

AR

OUTER
1
PARLOUR

2

The great seven-light window at the west end of the nave

windows that survive (but without most of their tracery) in all four gables of the church. Circular stairs in the north-west and south-west angles of the north and south transepts combined with a series of wall-passages gave access to all these roof-spaces, to the roofs themselves, and to the low bell tower that rose above the crossing.

In the north-west corner of the north transept is the *night-stair* by which the monks reached the church from their dormitory for the night-time services. The lower part of the six-light window, which did not clear the level of the roof of the monks' dormitory abutting its outer side, is treated as wall panelling.

The doorway in the north aisle of the presbytery gave access to the passage from the infirmary used by the elderly brethren to come to church.

The only tomb in its original position is that under the north arch of the crossing. The inscription reads: Hic : iacet : Nicholaus : Landaven-sis . . . (Here lies Nicholas of Llandaff). There was a Nicholas who was Precentor and Treasurer of Llandaff 1191–1218, and it is probable that he ended his days as a monk and this is his grave.

The monks, except at night-time, entered the church through the richly decorated doorway in the north aisle of the nave. This leads into the cloister.

Processional doorway leading from the cloister into the church

View from the south-west

Detail of west front, showing twin doorway, with elaborate tracery and wall panels

4 The *cloister* consisted of four passageways (now represented by gravel paths), covered by lean-to roofs set against the surrounding ranges of buildings, and built round a rectangular open court or garth. The walks were lit by a series of windows opening on to this garth and placed between the buttresses whose foundations remain. Fine examples of monastic cloisters still exist at, among other places, Westminster, Durham, Gloucester and Salisbury. The cloister not only provided covered access between the various parts of the monastery, but was used by the monks for study, especially the walk nearest the church. Here the remains of the canopied seat of the prior, who kept order, can be seen in the centre of the church wall. Normally the cloister was placed on the south side of the church so that it could get the sun. It was situated on the north side (as here at Tintern) only if drainage would otherwise have been difficult, or to secure greater privacy.

5 In the east cloister walk there is a round-headed recess with another blocked one beside it; these were the *cupboards* for books in use in the cloister.

The buildings round the cloister will now be described in turn.

6 The first doorway in the eastern range leads into a long room which was originally divided into two. The front part formed the *book room,*

Interior, looking towards the west window

Tintern Abbey as it might have appeared before the dissolution

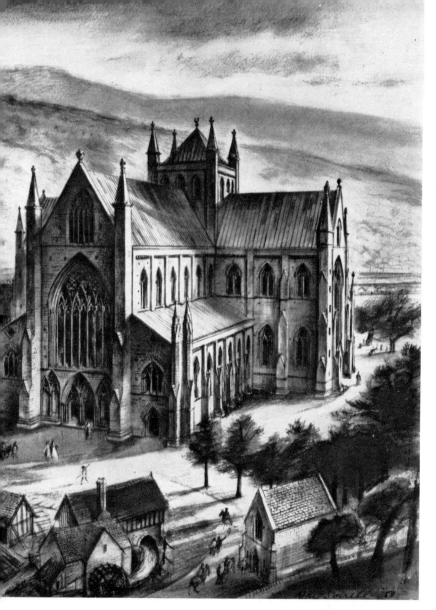

[Alan Sorrell, 1959]

Looking down the south aisle from the west front of the church

and the rear part, which was entered from the church, the *vestry*. Above the book room the line of the roof of the monks' dormitory, which occupied the whole of the first floor of the range, can be seen on the church wall.

7 The next room to the north is the *chapter house*. It took its name from the monks meeting there daily to hear a chapter of the rule of the Order read. Here also the monks discussed the business of the house, duties were allocated, faults confessed, and punishments decreed. The monks sat on a stone bench that ran round the sides of the room.

Air view from the north

The abbey church from the south-west

8 The chamber immediately north of the chapter house was the *parlour* where necessary conversation was allowed.

9, 10 The narrow space north of the parlour is believed to have contained the original *day-stairs* to the dormitory. North of this again is the *passage* leading from the cloister to the infirmary buildings.

11 On the north side of the passage, and occupying the remainder of the eastern range, is the *lodging for the novices* who comprised the new entrants to the monastery and who underwent a probationary period before graduating as monks.

12 Running eastwards at right angles to the novices' lodging is the *reredorter* or latrine. There would have been a row of cubicles set over the drain, possibly arranged on both first- and ground-floor levels. Water to flush the drain was led by culvert from a little stream that runs down the hillside to the north-west of the abbey precinct.

Visitors will probably find it most convenient next to look at the buildings on the north side of the cloister.

13 The archway near the north-east angle of the cloister leads into a vaulted passage on the east side of which is the doorway to the novices' lodging. Of the two arches at the north end of this passage, that on the left led into a yard, and that on the right to the site of the *day-stairs* to the monks' dormitory.

14 The first chamber to the west is the *warming house*. This was the only place, apart from the kitchen and infirmary, where a fire was allowed. There is a central fireplace, with all-round access to the fire. The rooms above were reached from the dormitory, and were occupied by the prior who was responsible for its discipline.

15 The large doorway opening off the centre of the north cloister walk is that of the *monks' dining hall*. There are two recesses on either side of the doorway: the larger contained the bowls where the monks washed before meals, and the smaller held the towels. The dining hall is 84ft long and 29ft wide. It was built in the early thirteenth century and replaced an earlier one which had run east and west. In the centre of its west side are the doorway and part of the stairs that led to the pulpit from which one of the brothers read aloud during meals. Near the south-east corner is a door leading to a pantry or storeroom, while close by in the south wall are a pair of recesses. The one on the left with a drain was for washing plates and spoons, and the other contained a cupboard for storing them. At the south end of the west wall there is a serving hatch from the kitchen, and, in the end wall nearby, the recess for a drop-down table.

16 The *kitchen* occupies the remainder of the north range. It served both the monks and the lay brothers: the latter's dining room was in the west range. The internal arrangement of the kitchen has been largely destroyed by the cottages which subsequently occupied its site.

It is probably easiest next to visit the infirmary and abbot's lodging, and, if time allows, look at the western range, in which the lay brothers had their quarters, on the way out.

17 The *infirmary* housed both the sick and the aged monks. Its buildings are reached through the passage at the north-east of the cloister.

The night-stair from the monks' dormitory

Water-colour drawing by J M W Turner

Cupboard for books in use in the cloister

The passage leads to the smaller infirmary cloister, and at the east end of its south walk is the infirmary hall. The hall, which is 107ft long and 54ft wide, was originally divided into a nave and aisles by two rows of columns. The inmates would have had their beds in the aisles and occupied the central part of the hall as their living room. In the fifteenth century the aisles were divided up into separate rooms each with its own fireplace.

18 The building to the north of the hall with a drain at its northern end is the *infirmary reredorter* or latrine.

19 The *infirmary kitchens* lie to the north of the hall. They date from the fifteenth century and must replace an earlier building. The massive lintel of the fireplace of one rests broken on the hearth, and the other has great fireplaces in its east and west walls.

The abbot's lodging is to the north of the infirmary. The head of a great monastic house had the administrative responsibilities of a feudal lord, and much of his time was occupied in furthering and protecting the interests of his house. He had a separate establishment in order that he could entertain important guests and come and go without upsetting the routine of the monks.

20 The building that runs east and west had the *abbot's camera* or living

room on the first floor. A doorway on the south side of this room led into the abbot's chapel.

21 The *abbot's hall* adjoins the "camera" on the west. Until recently its site was occupied by a cottage and its garden. The series of rooms now disclosed evidently formed storerooms and cellars under the hall, which was on the first floor.

22 As was normal in Cistercian houses, the western range had to accommodate the lay brothers as well as the storerooms, and consequently extends well to the north of the cloister. The *lay brothers' dining hall* was on the ground floor and their dormitory was above.

23 *The cellar*, the main storeroom of the abbey, lay to the south, and the cellarer, the official who was responsible for provisioning the monastery, had his lodging in the rooms above the parlour and its porch.

The Precinct. The area originally occupied by the abbey was considerably larger than it is today. It was enclosed by a wall, which on the west followed the line of the lane that runs behind the Beaufort Hotel—the present main road being an intrusion of about 1820.

The medieval gateway beside the Anchor Hotel led to the old ferry across the Wye. The foundations in the area west of the abbey church probably include those of the guest houses and mill.

View across the cloister showing the north transept and the line of the dormitory roof

Romantic study by Paul Sandby

The First Tourists

For nearly 200 years after the monks had been driven out few people other than those wishing to acquire building stone would have been interested in visiting the ruins of Tintern Abbey. In the sixteenth and seventeenth centuries wild scenery was generally regarded with dislike rather than affection. Furthermore with the introduction of classical architecture Gothic buildings were regarded as barbarous. The brothers Samuel and Nathaniel Buck, who visited so many of our ruined castles and abbeys in the early years of the eighteenth century, were amongst the first artists to take a systematic interest in medieval buildings (see page 3).

From about 1760 a few great houses began to be built in the neo-Gothic style. This led to a renewal of interest in medieval Gothic buildings. By this time they were mostly covered with a thick screen of vegetation,

Drawing by R Hancock of William Wordsworth at twenty-eight in the year he wrote his celebrated poem

and 'yonder ivy-mantled tower' was a subject for romantic rather than scientific study. Another factor was that, thanks to the more settled state of affairs at home and abroad, travel became considerably easier, and the roads, especially latterly, were greatly improved.

One of the first artists to draw English attention to the beauty of Welsh scenery and the picturesqueness of medieval remains was Paul Sandby, who first exhibited a drawing of Wales in 1773 (see page 26). So the first tourists began to arrive. The outbreak of the French Revolution sparked off the Romantic Movement, and, with the popularising of both wild scenery and the history of olden days, Tintern, like other ruins set in beautiful countryside, attracted a growing number of visitors.

William Wordsworth visited Tintern for the first time in the summer of 1793. His "Lines composed a few miles above Tintern Abbey on

View of the church from the south; the newel-stair in the angle of the transept gave access to the roofs

revisiting the banks of the Wye during a tour" were written five years later. Wordsworth said of it that "No poem of mine was composed under circumstances more pleasant for me to remember than this. I began it upon leaving Tintern, after crossing the Wye, and concluded it just as I was entering Bristol in the evening, after a ramble of four or five days (10–13 July) with my sister. Not a line of it was altered, and not any part of it written down till I reached Bristol." It was published that autumn (1798) in *Lyrical Ballads*, and was a landmark in poetic style. The opening lines, which so admirably conjure up the scene, are given below.

> Five years have past; five summers, with the length
> Of five long winters! and again I hear
> These waters, rolling from their mountain-springs
> With a soft inland murmur—once again
> Do I behold these steep and lofty cliffs,
> That on a wild secluded scene impress
> Thoughts of more deep seclusion; and connect
> The landscape with the quiet of the sky.
> The day is come when I again repose
> Here, under this dark sycamore, and view
> These plots of cottage-ground, these orchard-tufts,
> Which at this season, with their unripe fruits,
> Are clad in one green hue, and lose themselves
> Among the woods and copses, nor disturb
> The wild green landscape. Once again I see
> These hedgerows, hardly hedgerows, little lines
> Of sportive wood run wild: these pastoral farms,
> Green to the very door; and wreaths of smoke
> Sent up, in silence, from among the trees!
> With some uncertain notice, as might seem
> Of vagrant dwellers in the houseless woods,
> Or of some Hermit's cave, where by his fire
> The Hermit sits alone.

The drawing by J M W Turner (see page 23) was painted probably between 1790 and 1797 at a time when he was travelling 25 miles a day on foot making drawings of abbeys, cathedrals, bridges and towns.

An indication of the growing number of visitors is given by Charles Heath's *Historical and Descriptive account of the ancient and present state of Tintern Abbey* being in its eleventh edition by 1828. This guidebook points out that "two hours being the utmost limit that can be allowed

The south transept

company who make the excursion by water from Monmouth to Chepstow (by reason of the interference here of the tide), they would do right not to detain the boat at Monmouth," and "Boats for this pleasurable excursion are always in readiness at Monmouth and Chepstow." Alas that the same facilities are not available today!

Abaty Tyndyrn

Parodd ymlediad yr Eingl-Normaniaid i Gymru, yn anuniongyrchol o leiaf i fynachlogydd clas yr Hen Eglwys Geltaidd, ddiflannu'n gyfan gwbl, a daeth mathau eraill ar fywyd crefyddol i'r gymdeithas. Yn amlwg ymhlith y rhain yr oedd abatai'r Urdd Sistersaidd, y "mynaich gwyn," ac un o'r rhain oedd Tyndyrn. Sefydlwyd yr Abaty yma ym 1131 OC gan fynachod Ffrengig o L'Aumône yn Normandi, un o dai Citeaux yn Burgundy—prif dŷ yr Urdd. Bach oedd yr adeiladau cyntaf yn Nhyndyrn, ac fe'u hadeiladwyd gan mwyaf yn eu maint presennol yn y drydedd ganrif ar ddeg, a chwblhawyd eglwys yr abaty ym 1301. Ym 1536, gormeswyd y fynachlog gan Harri VIII pan ddiddymwyd tai crefyddol yn gyffredinol. Tynnwyd y plwm i ffwrdd a'i doddi, ac felly gadawyd y fynachlog yn fuan yn ei stad bresennol heb do. Perchennog preifat oedd iddo tan 1901 (Dugaid Beaufort), ac erbyn hyn mae'n eiddo'r Goron dan ofalaeth Adran yr Amgylchedd.

Adeiledid tai Sistersaidd ar gynllun pendant, er bod Tyndyrn yn wahanol i lawer gan fod yr adeiladau domestig ac adeiladau'r cwfaint, at ddibention traenio, i'r gogledd o eglwys yr abaty, yn hytrach nag i'r de yn ôl yr arfer. Safai'r amrywiol adeiladau a'r siambrau mewn patrwm pendant o amgylch pedair ochr garth hir sgwâr y clas (4), a byddai'r ystafelloedd cysgu ar y llawr cyntaf. Nodwedd ganolog y fynachlog oedd eglwys yr abaty (3) lle y treulid oriau yn ystod y dydd a'r nos yn addoli. Ar ôl ei orffen, yr oedd yn yr eglwys do bwaog gwych (noder bod rhai darnau o'r hen do yn awr ar y llawr), sgrîn yn gwahanu adran orllewinol corff yr eglwys a ddefnyddid gan y brodyr lleyg, a chorau deri gwych, mae'n debyg, ar gyfer y brodyr a fyddai'n canu ar ochr ddwyreiniol y sgrîn honno. Nodweddion o ddiddordeb arbennig heddiw yw rhwyllwaith y ffenestr orllewinol fawr yng nghorff yr eglwys, seiliau eglwys y fynachlog Normanaidd (wedi'u nodi ar y llawr) y porth addurniedig i'r eglwys o'r clas, bedd Nicholas o Landaf (yn ei safle gwreiddiol) ac, yn fwy na dim, y grisiau nos a ddefnyddid gan y mynachod i ddod i lawr o'u hystafelloedd gwely i'r swyddfeydd nos.

Rhodfa dan do oedd y clas yn wreiddiol (4) o amglch pedrongl agored y gellid darllen a myfyrio ynddo. Ohono eid i siambr (6) wedi'i rhannu'n ystafell lyfrau y tu allan a festri y tu mewn, ac o'r festri eid yn uniongyrchol i mewn i'r eglwys. Yn y cabidyldy (7) y trafodid unrhyw fusnes mynachol beunyddiol, dosbarthu'r dyletswyddau, a chywiro beiau. Yng ngwesty'r dysgwr (11) y trigai'r rhai a fyddai'n ymgymryd â chyfnod prawf llym cyn dod yn aelodau llawn o'r gymdeithas fynachaidd. Y tŷ cynhesu (14) oedd un o'r ychydig leoedd yn yr abaty y caniateid tân ynddynt. Safai'r gegin (16) yn gyfleus rhwng neuadd fwyta'r brodyr lleyg (22) a neuadd fwyta neu ffreutur y mynachod (15). Noder yn yr ystafell hon y pantri yn y cornel de-ddwyreiniol, yn agored i gludo'r bwyd o'r gegin, a'r grisiau i fyny i'r pulpud lle y byddai mynach yn darllen i'r gweddill yn ystod prydau bwyd.

Nid oedd yr ysbyty (17) ac ystafelloedd yr abad (20, 21) â chymaint o gysylltiad â'r clas. Yn yr adeiladau hyn, felly, gellid ymlacio o ddisgyblaeth fynachaidd heb amharu ar gorff y gymdeithas.

Yr oedd i'r ysbyty, ar gyfer y mynachod claf a hen ei chegin ei hun, gan y caniateid mwy o amrywiaeth bwyd i aelodau claf yr Urdd. Mae'n debyg y byddai'r ychydig ddyddiau ysbeidiol yn yr ysbyty ar gyfer gollwng gwaed yn ddigwyddiad pleserus i'r rhan fwyaf o fynachod Tyndyrn. Erbyn diwedd yr Oesoedd Canol, yr oedd abad Tyndyrn yn berson lled bwysig yn lleol a byddai gofyn iddo groesawu pobl a thrafod busnes. Tyfodd ei ystafelloedd, felly, i gryn faint gyda'u neuadd a'u capel eu hunain.

O gylch y fynachlog ganoloesol ceid mur y ffin—sylwer ar y porth canoloesol wrth Westy'r Anchor yn arwain at afon Gwy, a oedd yn bwysig i'r mynachod o ran trafnidiaeth. O fewn y ffin ceid gwesty lled fawr ar y darn tir sy'n ffinio â'r parc ceir.

Bu Abaty Tyndyrn yn atyniad cyson i lawer o ymwelwyr am dros ddau can mlynedd. Yn y dyddiau a fu, dôi rhai o'r rhain ar hyd Afon Gwy, ac eraill yn fwy diweddar ar y trên. Bu yma arlunwyr o fri (megis y brodyr Buck a J M W Turner) a bortreadodd yr Abaty ar gynfas; yr oedd un arbennig o'u plith yn fardd, William Wordsworth, ac anfarwolodd ef yr Abaty mewn cerdd. Erbyn hyn, yr ydych chwithau hefyd yn dilyn traddodiad cryf.

Printed in England for Her Majesty's Stationery Office by Swindon Press Ltd., Swindon, Wilts.

(739D) Dd. 496790 K360 7/76 Gp 469